Shades of a Woman

Shades of a Woman

Sara Rosete Hartel

RESOURCE *Publications* · Eugene, Oregon

SHADES OF A WOMAN

Resource Publications
An Imprint of Wipf and Stock Publishers
199 W. 8th Ave., Suite 3
Eugene, OR 97401

www.wipfandstock.com

PAPERBACK ISBN: 978-1-6667-8994-2
HARDCOVER ISBN: 979-8-3852-0006-1
EBOOK ISBN: 979-8-3852-0007-8

VERSION NUMBER 10/09/23

For Rubi, who never stopped trying to
make us better than she ever was

Contents

Acknowledgments

Thank you to all the family and friends that make my life so full. Special thanks to Cassie Holguin Pettinato and Vanessa Dremé for your fantastic editing skills.

A Woman in Scarlett

the coy muse

flittering

the eyes, the lips
some jabs, some nips
boys flitter and flatter

it lifts my gaze
I smirk back

and I'm drawn
on the tide of youth

beaming

I float on staccato swells
a ray of starlight
in a crowd of beaming stars

a million sparks

some days, I wish for a hundred
grand romances spanning my years
playfully weaving through my antics
sparks off flintstones
winking into the night

To #### and ####:

I thought about it
for a little while
where the strings of our lives
bounded and twined
our energies spark
but they should dance

A Woman in Indigo

what of a woman?

in her marrow

at first, she wants to be Jack Sparrow
aloof and snarky
deep in her marrow
she is Aragorn son of Arathorn
the honorable and brave
every scar, earned, shorn

and then, she wants to be Neil Caffery
slick and cunning
finding a way to be free
she is Tony Stark
witty and flippant
the center, the spark

and now, she won't let herself think
of being Jack, or Aragorn, or Neil, or Tony
since she's more of an ethereal Julia now
maybe a sultry Aubrey, or an adorable Meg
because in 2011 the flippant, butch girl
never finds love

and still, she wants them to adore her
for snark, for honor, for slick-backed wit
but, the Julias, Aubreys, and Megs always find love
the warm sleepy, soul crushing sort
a gooey, sugary treat to keep you sated

chummy

the lonely girl wears straight jeans
butch like a boy,
dutch like a dyke
she yearns to be chummy and rummy and carefree
the friendly girl now gets visitors all the time
some bring company and some bring gifts, and sometimes she
feels like it isn't all free
the price isn't comfort and chuckles, but attention, glimpses,
touches
underneath, she's still the lonely girl with her finger wedged in a
bulging,
burgeoning,
breaking dyke
the threatening Swell is murky with shame and smells of rotting
fish

she leads

She yells. Her voice lacks a certain timbre, a baritone inflection.

She stays silent. She stifles the vibrant flood of a thousand lived words—pinpointing a solution, conveying a truth, breathing a feeling.

She gives womanly kindness, caring, compassion; those are not womanly at all.

She makes jokes, takes quips. It's coquettish.

She is never quite one of the boys, or maybe she could be. They say she's unique, not like them, the gossipy, clingy, women.

She imagines she's the sun punching through the remnants of a harrowing thunderstorm. They see a crafty spider twisting words, luring pawns into her sticky trap.

girls and women

girls prove they are adventurous
women take brilliant risks

girls cling to the backs of men
women lead the pack

girls love to be loved
women love themselves

girls grow into women
women help grow girls

into women

trudge

I'm ashamed
of trudging after the line
slumped and bedraggled
handcuffed lovers
roles and expectations their jailers
while dances and chances flit by
a part of me detests that
I would fall in line
to fall in love

sundress

you only want to
talk about my
sundress
the dappled red
bouquet
the hem sliding
along mocha thighs
a buoyant step
when
the sheer fluttery
sleeves graze
my shoulders

but when you see my sundress,
you forget
I'm in it

A Woman in Gold

the coquettish friend

shivers

we're just kids, I'm sure it was a joke
when I heard you wanted
me dead
my eyelids froze
the chill of your resentment
evoked a shrunken shiver

I'm just the hollow bitch
who doesn't want you

twirling, unsecured

I crave
the attention,
the twirl and dip
energies tangling

I wretch
away from the judgment,
the shame
from being seen,
from doing
anything more than twirling

ghost faces line
the crowd
a name for each:
insecurity, wantonness, frivolity, shallowness

spoiled milk

our friendship curdles
in the stale air
nobody understands
my disgust with the awkward texts
the sour jokes, the lingering
looks
it's flattering isn't it?

smothered

I will not apologize
for clawing at the window
gasping for air

your attention
made me squeamish

morning coffee

"don't look" with your kind, lost eyes
at me
the shining woman
an incarnate inspiration on a pedestal

I'll take the coffee
it warms my crevices
I'll take the frothed oat milk
a creamy, steamy balm
the type I like
I'll take the texts, that lead into a joke
then a nudging buzz 3-4-5-6 a day
a sunrise ding,
a morning cup

"And, if I can't help but look?"
at the cinders coating the bottomless pit of a woman
a compliment, a coffee can't fill back up

and in my hand I offer my empty mug
where I scratched out my name and wrote hers

but I know all she'll get are ashes

To %%%%:

I couldn't be honest
since I couldn't be honest with myself
the claustrophobia crawling down my back
disgusted me, when I thought of being yours
so I fumbled our friendship, and for a while
it laid in dull shards on the ground

yesterday

we are two cobras circling
in a deadly dance
a cheap trick, some flowery words
and I'm a bandage
for your wound

it'll hurt her, I beg
just for tonight you say
I push you away
and voyage
to get out of this place

and I'll wake up ashamed
taking the blame
and you'll wake up and forget
all about
yesterday

A Woman in Coral

true friends are part of you

the odd and bold

you and me in the front seats.
the girls are heaped in the back.
here, in the darkness, we conjure our own world
the mountains beckon the odd and the bold
as the sun stretches over the foothills

To friends:

I hope you understand
how thankful I am
that you let me pull you across continents
and up mountains
I hoped to lead you to a warm campfire
with a flask and s'mores
but I know sometimes
it's a long, cold night and a million mosquitos

To————:

we were young
I was a catholic nun
my habit fluffed with righteousness and indignation
and I didn't see how I was trampling
you into dust

To ++++:

my memory crystallized
when you called to say
you were shamelessly happy
with a man
it surprised me
—

and, that thought hugged me
all day

To //////:

You've always been there
I am horrified
I did not realize you were sinking

Dear ####:

during the last few days of crying on and off,
I imagined our lives intertwining much longer
another ski trip,
another friend weekend or party
more singing, more laughing, more quirky outfits

flashbacks sear my brain
I think about how you could pull our group tight,
how you wanted to play guitar from a traveling van,
how happy you were to have found the love of your life-
how lucky we were to have you

love always

For my forever friend:

the rooftop facing the stars
the ledge of the hotel
those precious moments
of bickering and laughter
helped me
start to trust again
—

the brink of happiness
a taste of lightness

extrovert

it is electric
being around other people
I leap from the moon
dive through the atmosphere
and cannonball into
the mighty Pacific

questions

I want to be asked awkward questions
because I have so much to share

you might like my awkward questions
because you are worth sharing to

A Woman in Obsidian

the daughter

stubborn

when you looked at my lips,
you saw your twisted, snarling mouth
spewing flames
your stubborn bite
your mean streak
and the routine spiral
into a place where every face
is pale and ghoulish

last embers

I didn't like to see you like that
grotesque and bloated
when you were
as magnificent as a wildfire
on the mountain

but flames weren't meant
to burn forever

our reflection

I forgive you
at the bottom of your well
laid the soothing mother
clothed in fear and guilt
the creases in our hands
a warped mirror
the only thing left in the reflection
is love

The Translucent Woman

if it makes you uncomfortable, you care

head

I hate giving head

the first time, in the back of your truck
you pushed down my head

until I couldn't breathe
until I couldn't see

even when I tried to push you away
even when I clawed at your legs

I still hate giving head

stall

the broken yellow light
in the sticky bathroom stall
frazzles the monster trying to pry its way
out of my chest's crib
but my fingers can't seem to tap
the phone button

and I'm not sure
if I'm drunk or panicked
but I know what you did was wrong

rainbow waters

once I saw all the fish in the sea and the fish saw me,
sunlight struck shimmering scales
and we swam in rainbow waters
but now I'm just the hallway matte
I wish no one saw me

(revulsion)

blinders

my vision narrows
my feet moving
from class
to food
to my room

I hate
to admit
I'm scared to see him

debate

I debate
that it wasn't that bad
that I feel fine
that I'm strong enough to plow on
that much worse has happened to people
worse off
prolonged suffering, uncurable disease, years of watching your
family hurt
and I shift endlessly through my options
to let this pain sink away
to cut open the stitches
in hope of something
—

maybe nothing

release

sometimes I want to scream to release the guilt and stress
from the clutches of my mind

unresolved

I forced myself
to come here
the squat, brown office
of a lawyer
to see if anything could be done

a marathon trophy gleamed behind her
skeleton jaw
thin lips spitting words of acid:

"girls like you"
young pretty, party girls
"who laugh a lot"
and beckon the wrong type of attention

A Woman in Chartreuse

the other woman

To the boy who kept me from thinking about it:

you make me laugh
more than I have in awhile
and I'm a dice and you're a line of dominos
careening helplessly into your perfect life
but sometimes you
make me think
we could work

anhedonia

yesterday, late-night
I thought how
I left you in the freezing air
because it was warmer than my
frostbitten fingertips

you swore you weren't cold
but you were shaking
you *did* need that jacket
but I never even offered mine

is it wrong to say that I didn't want to?
I reach for your quivering hand
but it slips out of my
purple, shaky grip

**To the girl who loved the boy who
kept me from thinking about it:**

I should have noticed
because your feelings
were like pastel
flutterings
hoping
I want you both to be happy

later

I jut my jaw
years later
we still have our playful tension
and you're drawn to me
a moth to a flame
I know—even if she's
right there

I clench my teeth
because the stories
you've built
around yourself,
about us
don't mirror mine
a shining knight saving a weeping princess

A Woman in Slate

the muted woman

busy

I'm busy
I'm busy not thinking
I'm busy not feeling
I'm busy trying leap from this hole

but it just yawns and stretches

slippery grip

I have some helping hands
trying to help me stand
but I sink back
down
down
down
into the dark

I have some helping hands
they grip my arms
but I don't know how to hold on

doors

depression's door is homey and squat
milk shutters cover blackout curtains
and often people curl up inside

anxiety's door is shiny and slick
the windows high and wide
and often people peer at the circus inside

the house lights are so inviting at night
but I'm glad I couldn't stay

motionless

I am lucky my emotions move fast
I get obsessed when I sit still
motion is freedom

sitting in my head

there's a space
just for me

for endless hours wandering
to climb alone
to dance in silence
to gaze at everything unimpressed

to sit alone
in my bunk
with my companion, sadness

alone

I ran today
along the beach
to see the sunrise,
instead of friends
because my obsessions,
my hurt pride,
my lost love,
my looming ghoul,
ensnared me into
their tantalizing reservoir

blind

I want her back
the girl with the trusting smiles
and boundless energy

but the woman looking
is blind with rage

scream

where the darkness yawns
there is room to grow
there is room to scream
there is room for change

A Woman in Cerulean

fear deserves a laugh

soothe

revenge soothes
but reflection
is a gift
to yourself

now what?

I thought it would be like cutting melted butter
to look for retribution

but you apologized
now what?

for awhile
I felt like enduring your cuts and mine
just made Atlas want
to throw the world from
her shoulders
and sink into vapor

crack

when I was ready,
I chose forgiveness
and the floodgates cracked
in my mind

dance again

my hair swishing against my back to the flow of my body
it is good to dance again

slow roll

I know
I get a little bit better
everyday

worries, little bristles
still prick me
but I don't let them cling

just pick them off
and sweep them away

love, xxxx

I needed to learn
to love myself again

last winter's snow

I know I have a long way to heal
but right now
I know
I can still be who I dreamed
a sapling breaking through last winters' snow

stream

healing is not a tide
or a tsunami
it's a stream
that bounces and weaves
into a river
until it rests in a pool
creating a ripple

A Woman in Saffron

young love

stone blue

the first thing
I noticed
about you was
your stone blue eyes
you joked with me
and I wanted to know you

hope, punctured

I didn't tell anyone
that I bawled
on the shower floor

because I let myself
think it was more

first home

when you wrap your body
around mine
it warms my lower spine
I feel at home

us

I don't want to skate over
our struggle to find us

how I envisioned we would be

I have too many happy places
to choose just one
samba and coffee mornings
are a gift to myself

windswept mountain sunrises
to behold the expanse

the harmonized tango of making blueberry pancakes in the kitchen
with you

dressy, spring brunches
with my quirky people

and snuggling deep into your body
under a pile of snowy white covers

waking up in a new place
and the strange excitement that fills me

balm

I don't care how much us hurts
if the balm
still soothes

goldfish

I still remember the golden moments:
when you handed me colors
and caressed my shoulder
under the slice of friendly sun
where we painted goldfish

lose yourself

my mind is a glossy pool
its easy for her to pour in
doubts
for him to fan some ripples
for me to absorb you
until it's just you
and I-
evaporated

lovely me

I forgot
how to be lovely me

I forgot that I could be fine
without
you

graying

I wish you'd look at me
not your phone

straight into my pupils
and focus on us
on the gray couple
jibbering and jabbering
next to us in this café
and the feel of my hand in
yours

mountain top

sad music makes us clutch
each other tighter
leaves us skittish fools
fears and futures aren't good
either

we punctured a
dream
and kicked it
down the last eight pitches
of the mountain
we built
around the bend in the trail
and back into the parking lot
go home, try with some other
moony-eyed fools

but the dream is scrappy and
honestly quite cute
it's too hard to leave behind

clasp

green sparkling water
canoes and campers
you and me
idle waves roll us on the
edge of the dock
as we laugh
through the agonizing
tedious
process of
prying ourselves apart

the first break

I think my hysterical crying
has really worn me out

please get me a blanket and some tea

kindness or love

my emotions are riding me
when you drive me to
comforting Filipino food
when you hold me on an
overlook
when you keep me together
through my tears
when you bring me the extra
blanket
it makes me think
you're perfect for me

evaporating dreams

there's a doodle
on my letter
to you
it has a cabin
and a porch
with a garden for you
and mountains for me

Amber

deep down
I never thought we'd ever . . .
maybe I knew
we found a fork in the road

I think of the last month,
on the edge of the mountain
lake,
when you said we'd find each
other some day

I think of last week,
during a late-night call,
when you said you slept with
Amber

my heart

somewhere in the recesses of
my mind
I want you to gather me close
and to see my love splayed out
as a wonderfully complex
painting
and not the shriveled innards of
a dying game

pink park perch

sat on my pink park bench
for the morning sun
I let my thoughts run
I don't feel so jumbled anymore
only lost a continent away
you know I can't love you
anymore
I can't just start loving again
I'm stuck here, sick of loving at
all

Sat on my pink park perch
in the dappled noon
hoping to find my old self soon
before I understood that
the right fit is not easy to find
and we wouldn't work
now or ever
and I can't stop caring
now or ever

sat on my pink park perch
late into the evening light
shrunken heart not even willing
to fight

scramble

soothing each hand
feels easier
than scrabbling at scree
to keep me aloft

your needles

a rosy balloon
I've inflated
to cushion me with
new places and faces
the cascade of life

I've been dodging your needles
the pictures of you and someone
new
the laughing videos of you
the itch of waiting
for a text that never comes

I desperately need a thicker
balloon
but that's not how balloons
work

A Woman in Chardonnay

good lovers make bad friends

thunder

I feel the stillness
the pending snap
of a warm thunderstorm
of the quiet strain
in learning to be friends
over a juicy, red snapper
on the grill and sweet potato chips
in the fryer

bad nights

bad nights hurt
so brightly that you feel alive
a knife slicing through water

blurs of neon friends and good bars
laughing for the first time in a long time feels rusty
up late excited for a friend to text back
rushing along the precipice of youth
everything behind you is in ashes
but you keep running to the expanse

standing on a cliff's edge
screaming into the churning sea
where the water touches the stars

indulgence

it's enticing
to look up
see your eyes molten
to smirk, stare a second too long

but oh hell on earth no
the words I speak are
etched in stone
I'm indulgent, perhaps
not leading you on

A Woman in Champagne

the lost, hopeful, and happy settler

touché, life

the thing about him is
he makes me feel shiny
and polishes off the rust
with spontaneous kisses
unasked praises

that he's still a kite in the wind
the chain yanking an opening door
and doesn't trust people
just like me
but the main thing
is he wants 3–6 babies
a house with a southern belle
to whisper his name in his ear

and my thing
is that I want to run until
I catch the sky
touché, life

groggy

in the muted hours
we laze into our own world
limbs crisscross
snaking through blankets
groggy talking
languid teasing
happiness like
morning dew
blooming into existence
to trickle away with the day

fleeting

how can something
so light, so happy
be wrong for us?
how can I capture this kindness
and not capture you?
how can I hold you in my arms
if you'll just drain away
through my open palms?

A Woman in Lavender

early mornings, busy days, late nights

.

minds eye

Colorado grips my mind
an icy gale buffets me with loving arms,
heralding
echoes of wind-swept crags
down below
scraggy pines jut from
granite obelisks that pierce
bluebird skies

ache

when I'm still
on a gloomy morning
I brush the mist with my fingertips
a distant cerulean patch
makes my dusty veins
ache
to be a roaring river

behold, she rises

follow me into the horizon
on the way we might discover
how a mountain pierces the sun
when she rises

clearing

only you know why you are out here
with your heart and your head
a star chasing the sunrise

the mysteries of the wilderness
an elixir, a clearing
between the looming pines

baking away

I need more
than baking on crusty sandstone.
than lazy days
in smooth tunes.
I cocoon
my slow heap
of withering flesh
under the unrelenting sun.

eagle flight

foot hand foot hand
a moment of perfect nothingness
circling my brain

foot hand hand foot
I'm an eagle perched on an austere spire
giddy as a burst of wind
my fearless heart envelops everything below

reach, balance, pull
a gush bolsters my pride
a rush racing me skyward

Just foot foot hand foot
teetering
on the knife's edge

nerve

nerves show
you what you are excited to do
not what you fear

photograph

I can't quite capture the magnitude
or the sorrow that
one person
one family
one community
can endure

A Woman in Silver

finding future me

.

watercolor canyon

splatters of bodies and conversation
clutter the watercolor canyon walls
a crinkled foil beams from the gravel

a twisted sage longs for
the wind rushing through these empty halls
the perfect portrait cloaked in solitude

next to her
a jovial family jockeys for the first glimpse
of this masterpiece
the woman almost smiles

places and people

it's not about the things I do
or the places
I go
it's about how I learned
and who was there to learn with me

aloof

it's awkward to admit
you're getting old
that you're aloof from
the burgeoning of youth
you look on amused
at the careful crawl
from strangers to laughter
from simple touches to meaningful glances

like putting on a sweater and having
your sleeves stuck up at
your elbows
but the realizing it fits

pictures

when I see each picture
an old timey video rewinds and
my stories play out in my head
it makes me smile

dust

dust on my keyboard
rust on my mind
you never know
to treasure
the time when you
feel you that spark in your eyes
you could bounce off gravity

my brush

the best songs have
blank notes enough
to make a just outline
in your mind but you fill in the details
with your own brush

crows feet

in the mirror
my belly
balloons out, a protruding prong
another year, another pound
skates away from me
I wish I would, could
ignore the calories
and drink and gorge
in the halls
of Dionysus
laughing until it hurts
I wish I could, would
admire my
crows feet
until they became smiles lines
scars hewn from
a life savored

A Woman in Daffodil

I wake up excited because I have
so much more to give

.

teeter

some people teeter between two worlds
but the ridgeline helps me find my balance

moguls of life

absorbing bumps and waves,
molding to the mountain,
is more exhilarating than
flying through the air

a scrape on crust,
a puff of powder,
sparkles in the buttery light

spirit

if you give a little to the Earth,
she will let your spirit fly

rainy street

a sunny roof and friends
3pm on Rainy Street
lounging, spinning, singing
my world is a blur
my heart a smile
then I'm dancing
to a guitar and a man that sings wagon wheel
then we've met some people
on the grass, in the bathroom line,
and I'm not sure why they're so fun
my most ecstatic moments
in a bathroom line
needing to pee

shed

I think its time
to give myself to
others
and to the Earth

I have shed enough skin
to see my core

blatant heart

these hands are helping hands
because they are connected
to my blatant heart

horizon

the horizon gapes at me
and I smile back